About Mastering Basic Skills—Listening Skills:

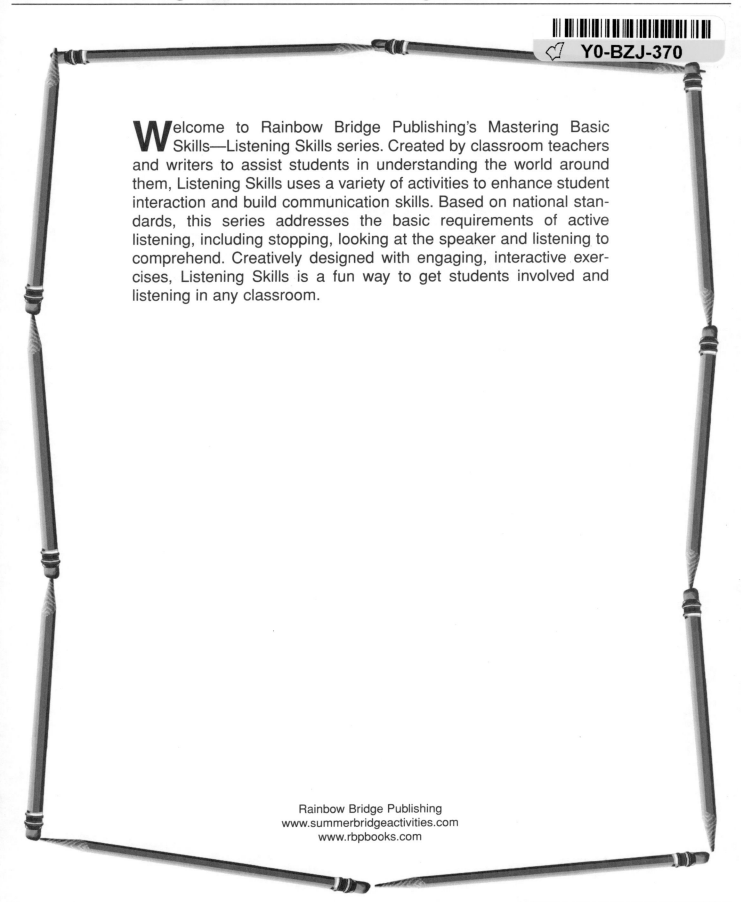

Welcome to Rainbow Bridge Publishing's Mastering Basic Skills—Listening Skills series. Created by classroom teachers and writers to assist students in understanding the world around them, Listening Skills uses a variety of activities to enhance student interaction and build communication skills. Based on national standards, this series addresses the basic requirements of active listening, including stopping, looking at the speaker and listening to comprehend. Creatively designed with engaging, interactive exercises, Listening Skills is a fun way to get students involved and listening in any classroom.

Rainbow Bridge Publishing
www.summerbridgeactivities.com
www.rbpbooks.com

Listening Skills • Table of Contents

◇ **Start Here!**

Teacher: Write the four steps for good listening listed below on the chalkboard. Read the story and the instructions aloud to the students.

Rob was sad because all the kids in his class had brought in shoe boxes for a special project they were starting at school. That is, all but Rob! "What happened?" asked Ms. Hansen. "You never forget to bring your supplies to school."

"I guess I wasn't listening when you were telling us about the box," said Rob. Ms. Hansen handed Rob a shoe box she had hidden beneath her desk and said, "Roberto, you need to practice your listening skills."

"Thanks for the box," said Rob. "I'll try to remember to use the four steps for good listening the next time you give instructions."

Here is what Rob did when Ms. Hansen began to tell the class how to decorate their shoe boxes.

S: He <u>stopped</u> what he was doing.

E: He <u>emptied</u> his hands of anything he was holding, such as pencils, erasers, books or paper.

L: He <u>looked</u> at the person who was speaking, Ms. Hansen.

L: He carefully <u>listened</u> and raised his hand to ask questions if there was something he didn't understand.

Write the four steps for good listening skills in their correct order:

_____ Listen

_____ Stop

_____ Empty

_____ Look

◇ **Start Here!**

Teacher: Make a copy of the picture on the next page for each student. Then read the story and the questions aloud to the students.

Rob raced home to tell his dad about the cool ladybug project he had made at school. By the time he reached home his heart was thumping so hard Rob could actually feel it beating inside his chest. "Boy, I'm out of breath," he said, plopping down on a kitchen chair.

"Relax and take deep breaths," his dad said as he bounced Rob's baby brother up and down. "You'll be just fine."

---

1 Did you know that a first grader's heart beats about 90 times every minute? Write the number 90 on the refrigerator door.

2 The sound of your heart pumping blood to the rest of your body is called the heartbeat. Color the heart on the cookie jar RED.

3 Your heart is almost the size of your fist. Make a fist with one hand. That is the size of your heart. Now circle Rob's fist in ORANGE.

4 Your heart is the most important muscle in your body. If you don't give it exercise, it will become soft and flabby. Put a STAR on Rob's chest.

5 Exercise, like running, helps your heart to get the oxygen it needs to stay healthy. Think about what you do for exercise every day, then color Rob's shoes PURPLE.

6 Eating good foods such as fruits, vegetables and whole grains helps your heart stay strong. Color the banana YELLOW.

7 Foods with lots of fat in them, like ice cream, potato chips or hot dogs, can clog the tubes, or blood vessels, that bring oxygen to your heart. Put an X on the cube of butter.

8 Sometime today, surprise your friends and tell them that some insects have green or blue blood. They might not believe you, but it's true! Now color the beetle hiding under the table BLUE and GREEN.

Name _____　　　Date_____

Name _____ Date_____

◇ **Start Here!**

Teacher: See page 32 for directions.

◇ Start Here!

Teacher: Read the instructions and the story aloud to the students.

I'm going to hand you a piece of paper. When you get it, write your first and last name on the top line. Next, write the numbers 1–5 down the left-hand side of the paper. Then, put your pencil down and get ready to listen to a story.

One fine spring day a fat, brown grasshopper was chirping and singing in the woods. Suddenly, he noticed a tiny, black ant carrying a small, green pea back to its nest. "Hey, Ant," said Grasshopper. "Instead of working so hard, why don't you come and sing with me?"

"I'm helping my family gather food for the winter, and if you knew what was good for you, you would be doing the same," answered Ant.

"Don't be silly," replied Grasshopper. "Winter is months away, and I want to enjoy myself before the snow falls again."

The little ant just nodded his head and went back to work. All too quickly the hot summer turned to a golden fall, and then one cold morning, Grasshopper woke to find snow dusting his wings. "Oh, no!" thought Grasshopper. "I'm in trouble now!"

Listen closely as I read each question; then write the letter that gives the best answer.

1. What color was the pea?
    A. brown   B. green   C. black

2. What season was it when Grasshopper said, "Come sing with me"?
    A. fall   B. winter   C. spring   D. summer

3. Why was Ant taking the pea back to his nest?
    A. He was hungry and wanted it for lunch.
    B. His mom was making split pea soup.
    C. He was going to store it away for winter.

4. Why did Grasshopper say, "I'm in trouble now?"
    A. He hadn't listened to Ant and didn't have food gathered for the winter.
    B. He had planned to borrow food, but he forgot where Ant lived.
    C. His wings were frozen shut, and he couldn't fly.

5. Write a new title for "The Ant and the Grasshopper."

_____

Tidy Habitats 🐝

◇ **Start Here!**

Teacher: Make a copy of the picture on the next page for each student. Then read the story and the questions aloud to the students.

Rob was lying on his bed holding a copy of <u>Insects</u> by Margo Smith. Ms. Hansen had talked to the class about habitats. She said that habitat means "a place where a living thing lives." After Ms. Hansen had read "The Ant and the Grasshopper," Rob decided he was more like Ant than Grasshopper because he liked to be organized, just like an ant. He opened his book and started to read more about ants.

---

1 Rob's favorite color is light blue. Color the wall by his space poster LIGHT BLUE.

2 Most ants make their nests underground. Draw a SQUARE under the window.

3 The common black ant's nest is made up of rooms connected by tunnels. Color the drawers on Rob's desk YELLOW and ORANGE.

4 Each room, or chamber, is kept clean by a worker ant. Think about what you can do to keep your room clean. (Pause) Now put an X on the paper next to Rob's bed.

5 Parasol ants chew parts of leaves off plants and carry them back to their nests. <u>Parasol</u> means umbrella, and these little ants look like they are holding umbrellas over their heads. Color the umbrella BLACK.

6 Ants are always looking for bits of food, even in your house. Draw a TRIANGLE around the candy bar in the window.

7 Did you know that some caterpillars spit out a juice like honey that black ants drink? The black ants say thank you by biting any other insects that try to hurt the caterpillar. Color Rob's baseball bat BROWN.

8 Ants, like all insects, have six legs. Write SIX on the closet door.

9 Count how many ants are in Rob's room and write that number on his book.

Name _____   Date_____

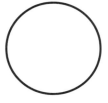

⬦ **Start Here!**

Teacher: Sing these chants many times in class, at different times and on different days. As students master the movements, place a sticker or a stamp in the circle.

In the Sky
Put your thumb in the sky, in the sky
Put your thumb in the sky, in the sky
Put your thumb in the sky,
Oh my, it's way too high
Put your thumb in the sky, in the sky
(finger, elbow, nose, ear, foot, knee, toe)

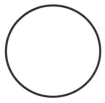

K-I-T-T-Y-O
There was a boy who had a cat
and Kitty was her name-o.
K-I-T-T-Y, K-I-T-T-Y, K-I-T-T-Y
and Kitty was her name-o.

There was a boy who had a cat
and Kitty was her name-o.
[Clap]-I-T-T-Y, [clap]-I-T-T-Y, [clap]-I-T-T-Y
and Kitty was her name-o.
etc.

There was a boy who had a cat
and Kitty was her name-o.
[Clap-clap-clap-clap-clap,]
[Clap-clap-clap-clap-clap,]
[Clap-clap-clap-clap-clap]
and Kitty was her name -o.

(Pick new people to put in place of the boy. Pick five-lettered animals such as doggy or piggy, and play again.)

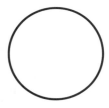

Jump to the Rhythm
Jump to the rhythm;
jump, two, three.
Jump to the rhythm;
clap, two, three.

Jump to the rhythm;
turn to the right.
Jump to the rhythm;
turn to the left.

Jump to the rhythm;
turn to the left.
Jump to the rhythm;
turn to the right.

Jump to the rhythm;
turn all around.
Jump to the rhythm;
sit yourself down.

(This is done to a simple chant. After the word "jump," in all the lines that read "jump to the rhythm," the students should jump. Then, just follow the chant's directions.)

⬦ **Start Here!**

Teacher: Read the instructions and the story aloud to the students.

I'm going to hand you a piece of paper. When you get it, write your first and last name on the top line. Next, write the numbers 1–5 down the left-hand side of the paper. Then, put your pencil down and get ready to listen to a story.

The wind and the sun were fighting about who was stronger. Suddenly, they saw a man walking down the road. Sun said, "I know a way to decide who is stronger. Whoever can make that man take off his coat wins. You try first." And Sun disappeared behind a dark cloud.

Wind began to blow as hard as it could. The harder Wind blew, the tighter the man held onto his coat. Finally, Wind could blow no more and had to rest. Sun moved out from behind the cloud and began to gently shine down on the man. Sun shined and shined until the man was warm, then hot, then finally took off his coat.

Listen closely as I read each question; then write the letter that gives the best answer.

 Who was fighting?
- A. Sun and the man
- B. Sun and Wind
- C. Wind and the man

 What did the man do when Wind blew?
- A. covered his eyes
- B. wished the clouds would go away
- C. pulled his coat closer to him

 Where did Sun go while Wind blew?
- A. behind a cloud
- B. behind a mountain
- C. behind a tree

 Who was the strongest?
- A. Wind
- B. Sun
- C. The man

 Write a new title for "The Wind and the Sun."

Teacher: Make a copy of the picture on the next page for each student. Then read the story and the questions aloud to the students.

"Mom," said Rob as he handed a piece of paper to his mother. "Look at this! I have a math test tomorrow." Mom stopped reading her book and looked at the piece of paper that Rob's teacher had sent home.

"Oh, Roberto," said Mom. "You don't need to worry. You can do all these problems."

"But, Mom, we don't get to look at the problems. Ms. Hansen tells us the problems aloud. We need to listen carefully, and sometimes I'm not very good at that."

"That's OK, Roberto. Let's just practice."

---

1 It's five o'clock. Show that TIME on the clock.

2 What is two plus three? Write that number on the lamp.

3 Roberto's mom had four library books. She took two back to the library. How many library books does she have now? Color that many BOOKS on the bookshelf.

4 Find the number 47 hidden in the picture. Color it BLUE.

5 Write the number that is <u>more</u> on the paper in Mom's hand: 27 or 72.

6 Write the number that is <u>less</u> on the book next to Mom: 13 or 18.

7 Find the dollar sign hidden in the picture and put an X on it.

8 Color the outside ring on the rug GREEN.

9 Color the next ring ORANGE.

10 Color the last ring YELLOW.

Name _____ Date_____

◇**Start Here!**

Teacher: Read the instructions; then read the directions aloud to the students.

Paper-folding, or origami, is an excellent tool for teaching listening skills. It requires the child to both look and listen carefully as the teacher demonstrates each step. Allow plenty of time for each step.

The puppy is the easiest of all origami folds. Children usually want to practice this over and over as their confidence builds. Have them name each of the puppies in their litter and provide a basket (a brown paper bag, rolled down) to keep all their creations safe.

---

1 Start with a paper square (8" x 8").

4 Fold up the top sheet of the bottom corner to make a mouth and nose.

2 Fold in half, corner to corner.

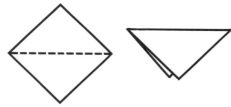

5 Color on a nose, tongue and two eyes.

3 Fold down the corners to make the ears.

◇ **Start Here!**

Teacher: Follow the instructions below. See page 32 for answers.

Read the riddles aloud and have students write their guesses down on a piece of paper. (This allows everyone a chance to think of an answer.) After the answer is revealed, pair up the students to write their own riddles.

The riddles may then be read in class. Also, have the students illustrate their riddles for display in the hall. Of course, for fun you would leave off the answers.

It lives in the winter.
It dies in summer.
And it grows with its roots up.

Twenty white horses on a red hill.
First, they chomp and chomp.
Then, they stand still.

It runs all day and never walks.
It often murmurs, never talks.
It has a bed but never sleeps.
It has a mouth but never eats.

It has a trunk
And moves with the wind.
It doesn't have a head
But has lots of limbs.

It's white as snow.
It's yellow as the sun.
You can bake it in a birthday cake
For lots of fun.

◇ Start Here!

Teacher: Make a copy of the picture on the next page for each student. Then read the story and the questions aloud to the students.

"Look at this!" said Rob as he plunked a library book down on Ms. Hansen's desk. "I'll never be able to paint like this guy."

Ms. Hansen opened the book and smiled. "This is an art book about Claude Monet. He was a famous painter who lived in France over 100 years ago. Maybe when he was little he wanted to be a veterinarian just like you. Would you like to learn more about him?"

"Sure!" said Rob. "But, I don't think he wanted to be a veterinarian."

---

1 Claude Monet was a French painter who helped start a new way of painting. Underline his name in BLACK.

2 Instead of making his painting look exactly like what he saw, he used bright chunks of paint that he would smash onto the canvas. Fill in the frog with dots or chunks of GREEN.

3 Before Monet and his painter friends started painting, most pictures were dark with lots of gray, brown and black in them. Color the picture frame YELLOW.

4 Monet lived in a pink and green house in a town north of Paris, France. Put a P in the bottom-left corner of the picture frame.

5 Monet lived in this house with his eight children and Alice, his wife. Write the number 8 in the upper-right corner of the picture frame.

6 Monet painted many different things, but he is most famous for his water lilies, sunflowers and vases filled with flowers. Color the flower PURPLE.

7 Monet and his gardeners planted a garden so he would have plenty of flowers to look at while he painted. Color the water in the pond BLUE.

8 The garden had a pond where his water lilies grew. Color the lily pad PINK. It is under the purple flower.

9 There was also a bridge where visitors could stand and enjoy looking at all the beautiful flowers. Color the bridge BROWN.

Name _____ Date _____

CLAUDE
MONET

Name _____   Date_____

◇ **Start Here!**

Teacher: See page 32 for directions.

◇**Start Here!**

Teacher: Read the instructions; then play the game with your students.

Copy and cut out the cards on pages 17–18. If you want the cards to be sturdier, glue them to card stock and laminate.

Place the cards in a container and have a student pull a card and read the directions. All the students follow the directions until the next card is read. These cards work well for Simon Says. However, instead of Simon, use the name of a person you are currently studying in the classroom (i.e., Monet, Ben Franklin, Martin Luther King). Students should all be standing.

Jump on one foot.	Clap your hands three times.
Jump on two feet.	Put both thumbs together.
Put your hand on top of your head.	Touch your nose.
Wave your left hand.	Sit down.

Touch your right thumb to your nose; then close your eyes.	Sit down; then stand up.
Turn completely around and sit down.	Put both hands on your knees and jump up once.
Wiggle your fingers and put your left foot forward.	Put your left hand on your head and jump on your right foot.
Put your right hand on your head and jump on your left foot.	Put your hands over your ears and hop three times.

◇ **Start Here!**

Teacher: See page 32 for directions.

Pussy Cat and
the Queen

"Pussy-cat, pussy-cat,
where have you been?"
"I've been to London
to look at the Queen."

"Pussy-cat, pussy-cat,
what did you do there?"
"I scared a little mouse
under the chair."

Wee Willie Winkie

Wee Willie Winkie went
through town.
Upstairs and downstairs,
in his nightgown.
Rapping at the windows,
crying through the lock.
"Are the children
in their beds?
For now it's eight o'clock."

Georgy Porgy

Georgy Porgy,
pudding and pie,
Kissed the girls
and made them cry.
When the boys came
out to play,
Georgy Porgy ran away.

Baa, Baa, Black Sheep

"Baa, baa, black sheep,
have you any wool?"
"Yes, sir. Yes, sir.
Three bags full.
One for my master,
One for my dame,
And one for the little boy
Who lives down the lane."

◇ **Start Here!**

Teacher: Make a copy of the picture on the next page for each student. Then read the story and the questions aloud to the students.

"Boys and girls, now is a good time to review how a person can practice listening skills," said Ms. Hansen. "All of you have been working hard to listen and follow directions."

"Ms. Hansen," Rob said. "I always try to remember the word SELL. It reminds me of the four steps to good listening."

"You're right! S for stop, E for empty hands, L for look at who's talking, and L for listen carefully. Let's practice."

---

1. Solve the math problem on the blackboard.

2. Circle the third letter of the alphabet in BLACK.

3. Circle the word on the blackboard that rhymes with BAT.

4. Find a pyramid, or triangle shape, and color it ORANGE.

5. Draw a STAR on the sphere, or ball.

6. Circle the second to last letter of the alphabet in RED.

7. Write your PHONE NUMBER on the blackboard.

8. Put two SCOOPS of ice cream on top of the cone.

9. Color the scoops PINK and GREEN.

10. Draw a LINE under the cube, or square shape.

Name _____   Date_____

abcdefghijklmnopqrstuvwxyz

◇Start Here!

Teacher: Read the instructions; then read the directions aloud to the students.

The rabbit is an easy origami animal to make. Here the students get more practice at both watching the speaker and listening to the instructions.

After they have mastered both the puppy and the rabbit, arrange for your class to teach other students, older or younger, it doesn't matter. Afterwards, discuss how the project went. Was it important for the people they were teaching to listen well?

---

1 Start with a square (8" x 8"), folded in half, corner to corner.

 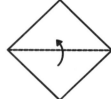

2 Fold up the creased edge about 1".

3 Fold up both outer points to form the ears.

4 Flip rabbit over and fold top point down.

5 Draw on eyes, nose and mouth. Color inside of ears.

◇ **Start Here!**

Teacher: Read the instructions and the story aloud to the students.

I'm going to hand you a piece of paper. When you get it, write your first and last name on the top line. Next, write the numbers 1–5 down the left-hand side of the paper. Then, put your pencils down and get ready to listen to a story.

There once was a rabbit so strong and fast that when he ran past other animals, all they saw was a white blur. "I have never been beaten in a race," bragged Rabbit. "I dare anyone in the desert to race against me."

Turtle spoke up and said quietly, "I will race against you."

All the desert animals burst into laughter, and the wise old owl said, "Dear Turtle, Rabbit will surely beat you."

"Let's wait and see," answered Turtle. "Shall we begin?"

So off they went. Rabbit darted out of sight at once, but being so sure he would win, he decided to stop and take a short nap. Turtle, however, plodded on and on, one foot in front of the other.

When Rabbit woke from his nap, he saw Turtle just in front of the finish line, and no matter how fast he ran, he could not beat the slow and quiet Turtle.

Listen closely as I read each question; then write the letter that gives the best answer.

1 Where did the race take place?
A. in the mountains
B. in the forest
C. in the desert

3 What color was Rabbit?
A. gray
B. white
C. brown

2 Who told Turtle that Rabbit would win?
A. the owl
B. the eagle
C. the fox

4 Why did Turtle win?
A. because Rabbit got lost
B. because Turtle didn't rest
C. because Turtle took a nap

Write a new title for "The Rabbit and the Turtle."

_____

> ◇ **Start Here!**
>
> Teacher: Make a copy of the picture on the next page for each student. Then read the story and the questions aloud to the students.

"Ms. Hansen, look at this! This book says penguins are birds, and seals are mammals," said Roberto. "Can we learn more about penguins?"

"No problem," answered Ms. Hansen as she reached for a book that explained the life of a penguin.

---

1 Penguins are birds. They have feathers and beaks, and they lay eggs. Draw a CIRCLE around a penguin egg.

2 Penguins look a bit like seals when they swim, but they are not related to seals. Put an X on the seal.

3 Penguins have been timed swimming at fifteen miles per hour. That is four times faster than the fastest human swimmer. Put the number 15 in the empty penguin nest.

4 When penguins are on land, they waddle slowly from place to place. However, if a penguin is afraid or angry, it will put its head down and run with surprising speed. Find the angry penguin.(Pause) Color its feet, back and head BLACK.

5 Penguins use their black and white colors to keep their body temperature just right. If a penguin is hot, it will turn its white belly to the sun to reflect the sun's heat away. Color the head of the hot penguin RED.

6 If a penguin is cold, it will turn its black back to the sun to soak up the sun's warmth. Color the feet of the cold penguin BLUE.

7 Sharks and leopard seals eat penguins. Color the shark GRAY.

8 Humans have brought cats and foxes to live near the penguins' habitats, or homes. These animals eat both live penguins and their eggs. Color the fox ORANGE. (Pause) Color the cat BROWN.

Note: All penguins live south of the equator, from the icy waters of Antarctica to the tropical coast of Ecuador.

Name _____ Date_____

◇ Start Here!

Teacher: Read the story and the instructions to the students.

Long ago, a large family of mice held a meeting to discuss what they could do about their enemy, the cat. Long into the night they argued over possible ways to defeat this terrible creature. Finally, a very young mouse stood up and said, "I think you will all agree that the greatest danger comes when she sneaks up on us on her silent paws. If we could hear her approach, we could easily escape. Therefore, I suggest we attach a ribbon with a bell around her neck. Then we would always know when the cat was in our neighborhood."

All the mice rose to their paws, cheering and clapping, until a very old mouse said, "Splendid idea! But tell me, who will put the bell on the cat?"

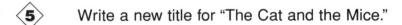

Listen closely as I read each question; then write the letter that gives the best answer.

1 The mice were in danger from
    A. other mice   B. birds   C. a cat

2 The mice were still arguing during the
    A. day   B. night

3 The cat was dangerous because she was
    A. silent   B. fast   C. hungry

4 Who offered to put the bell on the cat?
    A. the very old mouse
    B. no one
    C. the young mouse

5 Write a new title for "The Cat and the Mice."

_____

◇ **Start Here!**

Teacher: Read the instructions and the story to the students.

I'm going to hand you a piece of paper. When you get it, write your first and last name on the top line. Next, write the numbers 1–5 down the left-hand side of the paper. Then, put your pencil down and get ready to listen.

Once, when a lion was asleep, a little mouse happened to run over the top of the lion's paw. With a mighty roar, the lion woke and captured the mouse by its tail. As his big jaws opened to swallow the mouse, the tiny creature cried out, "Oh, King of the Jungle, don't eat me. Someday I may be able to do you a great favor." The lion was so amused by the thought of such a tiny mouse helping him that he lifted his paw and let the mouse go.

Sometime later, the lion was caught in a hunter's trap. The more he struggled to free himself, the tighter the net wrapped around him. Soon, the jungle was filled with the lion's terrible howl. Hearing the cry, the mouse raced to the net and began to chew away at the ropes. At last, when the lion was freed, he turned to the mouse and said, "I was wrong my little friend. Big is not always better."

Listen closely as I read each question; then write the letter that gives the best answer.

◇**1** The lion captured the mouse by its
   A. paws   B. tail   C. jaws

◇**2** The lion thought the idea of a mouse helping him was
   A. funny   B. smart   C. sad

◇**3** The mouse chewed on
   A. his paw   B. the lion   C. the rope

◇**4** Who was the King of the Jungle?
   A. the hunter   B. the mouse   C. the lion

◇**5** Write a new title for "The Lion and the Mouse."

_____

◇ **Start Here!**

Teacher: Make a copy of the picture on the next page for each student. Then read the story and the questions aloud to the students.

Rob always had fun when it was his turn to empty the classroom garbage cans at the end of the school day. However, today he was feeling bad. His uncle, who worked at the City Recycling Center, had told him just last night that we all need to do more to help the planet by recycling. "What can I do?" thought Roberto as he dumped a bunch of used paper into the giant hall cans. "I'm only a kid!"

---

1 A normal American family throws away about ten pounds of garbage each day. Color the smaller garbage can BROWN.

2 Have you ever wondered what happens to your garbage? Some gets burned, but most goes to your neighborhood dump. Color the fire RED.

3 If you put together all the garbage Americans throw away in one year, you would have a line of garbage trucks 145,000 miles long, or over halfway to the moon. Write 145 on the big garbage can.

4 Every year Americans throw away enough plastic soda bottles to encircle the earth four times. Color the soda bottle GREEN.

5 Every year Americans throw out enough white writing paper to build a wall from San Francisco to Boston ten feet high. Draw a LINE from one side of the map to the other. (Pause) Now write the number 10 in the middle of the map.

6 Every three months Americans throw away so many aluminum cans that all the airlines in the United States could rebuild every plane they own. Color the airplane BLUE.

7 Recycling just one glass bottle will save enough energy to light the lamp by your bed for four hours. Color the light bulb YELLOW.

8 Recycling just one aluminum can will save enough energy to run your TV for three hours. Color the soda can PURPLE.

Name _____ Date _____

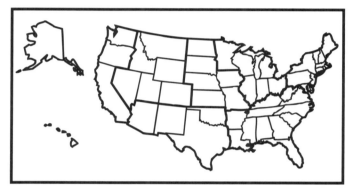

©Rainbow Bridge Publishing   www.rbpbooks.com   reproducible   **MBS—Listening Skills Grade 1**

Directions

PAGE 6: A Loony Ladybug

1. Color the ladybug's eyes RED.
2. Color the triangle with the circle GREEN.
3. Color two of the ladybug's spots PURPLE.
4. Color the triangle with the square ORANGE.
5. Color the circles on the ladybug's antennae BLACK.
6. Color five of the ladybug's spots BLUE.
7. Color the last five spots YELLOW.
8. Color the ladybug's legs BROWN.
9. Count how many spots the ladybug has and write that number on a cloud.
10. Count how many legs the ladybug has and write that on the other cloud.

PAGE 18: Starburst

1. Color the sun YELLOW.
2. Color the cloud BLACK.
3. Color two raindrops BLUE.
4. Color the following words PURPLE: Rob, and, but, Matt, if.
5. Color the following words ORANGE: the, Allie, to, Denise, so.
6. Color the diamond on the right RED.
7. Color the diamond on the left GREEN.

PAGE 21: Do you know…

Have the students number a paper 1 to 8; then ask the following questions after each poem:

Pussy Cat
1. Where did the cat go?
2. What did the cat scare?
Wee Willie Winkie
3. What time was it?
4. What was Willie wearing?
Georgy Porgy
5. Who did Georgy kiss?
6. Name one thing Georgy ate?
Baa, Baa, Black Sheep
7. How many bags did the sheep have?
8. What was in the bags?

Answers

PAGE 3: S.E.L.L

1. Stop (what you are doing).
2. Empty (hands of all objects).
3. Look (at the person who is talking).
4. Listen (and ask questions if needed).

PAGE 7: The Ant and the Grasshopper

1. B. green
2. C. spring
3. C. He was going to store it away for winter.
4. A. He hadn't listened to Ant and didn't have food gathered for the winter.
5. Answers will vary.

PAGE 11: The Wind and the Sun

1. B. Sun and Wind
2. C. pulled his coat closer to him
3. A. behind a cloud
4. B. Sun
5. Answers will vary.

PAGE 15: Riddles

an icicle, teeth, a river, a tree, an egg

PAGE 21: Do You Know Your Mother Goose?

<u>Pussy Cat</u>
1. London
2. mouse

<u>Wee Willie Winkie</u>
3. eight o'clock
4. night gown

<u>Georgy Porgy</u>
5. girls
6. pudding or pie

<u>Baa, Baa, Black Sheep</u>
7. three
8. wool

PAGE 25: The Rabbit and the Turtle

1. C. in the desert   2. A. the owl
3. B. white   4. B. because turtle didn't rest
5. Answers will vary.

PAGE 28: The Cat and the Mice

1. C. a cat   2. B. night
3. A. silent   4. B. no one
5. Answers will vary.

PAGE 29: The Mouse and the Lion

1. B. tail   2. A. funny
3. C. the rope   4. C. the lion
5. Answers will vary.

SBA Kids
Completion Award

Rainbow Bridge Publishing
Certificate
of Completion

Awarded to

_____

for the completion of

Mastering Basic Skills

George Stark.

_____   _____
Publisher's Signature   Parent's Signature

Summer Bridge Activities™

Title	Price
Grade P-K	$12.95
Grade K-1	$12.95
Grade 1-2	$12.95
Grade 2-3	$12.95
Grade 3-4	$12.95
Grade 4-5	$12.95
Grade 5-6	$12.95

Summer Bridge Middle School™

Title	Price
Grade 6-7	$12.95
Grade 7-8	$12.95

Summer Bridge Reading Activities™

Title	Price
Grade 1-2	$6.95
Grade 2-3	$6.95
Grade 3-4	$6.95

Summer Journal™

Title	Price
Summer Journal™	$4.95

Summer Dailies™

Title	Price
Summer Dailies™	$4.95

Summer Traveler™

Title	Price
Summer Traveler™	$4.95

Math Bridge™

Title	Price
Grade 1	$9.95
Grade 2	$9.95
Grade 3	$9.95
Grade 4	$9.95
Grade 5	$9.95
Grade 6	$9.95
Grade 7	$9.95
Grade 8	$9.95

Reading Bridge™

Title	Price
Grade 1	$9.95
Grade 2	$9.95
Grade 3	$9.95
Grade 4	$9.95
Grade 5	$9.95
Grade 6	$9.95
Grade 7	$9.95
Grade 8	$9.95

Skill Builders™

Title	Price
Phonics Grade 1	$2.50
Spelling Grade 2	$2.50
Vocabulary Grade 3	$2.50
Reading Grade 1	$2.50
Reading Grade 2	$2.50
Reading Grade 3	$2.50
Math Grade 1	$2.50
Math Grade 2	$2.50
Math Grade 3	$2.50
Subtraction Grade 1	$2.50
Subtraction Grade 2	$2.50
Multiplication Grade 3	$2.50

Connection Series™

Title	Price
Reading Grade 1	$10.95
Reading Grade 2	$10.95
Reading Grade 3	$10.95
Math Grade 1	$10.95
Math Grade 2	$10.95
Math Grade 3	$10.95

Mastering Basic Skills™

Title	Price
Grammar Grade 1	$5.95
Grammar Grade 2	$5.95
Grammar Grade 3	$5.95
Word Problems Grade 1	$4.95
Word Problems Grade 2	$4.95
Word Problems Grade 3	$4.95
Word Problems Grade 4	$4.95
Listening Skills Grade 1	$4.95
Listening Skills Grade 2	$4.95
Listening Skills Grade 3	$4.95

Math Test Preparation™

Title	Price
Math Test Prep Grade 1	$10.95
Math Test Prep Grade 2	$10.95
Math Test Prep Grade 3	$10.95

First Step Spanish™

Title	Price
Colors/Shapes	$5.95
Alphabet/Numbers	$5.95

Place Proper Postage Here

Rainbow Bridge Publishing
PO Box 571470
Salt Lake City, Utah 84157

Keeping Children Busy, Happy, and Learning During the Summer and Beyond!